I Wish You Bluebirds

By Mary Alice Loberg

Illustrated by Marilyn Conklin

HALLMARK EDITIONS

I Wish You Bluebirds

I wish you Bluebirds
All the year
through...

Bluebirds of joy
For the things that you do...

And a warm hand to hold
In the closeness of dark.

Frosty night hayrides
Through the park

A marshmallow roast
With friends down the street...

Crisp leaves
To scrunch with your feet...

In the AUTUMN,
When summer is gone,
May you have bluebirds
And bright golden dawns...

And whenever it's cloudy
And you're feeling sad,
May someone share memories
Of good times you've had.

In the SUMMER,
On hot thirsty days,
May you have bluebirds
And pink lemonades...

Bluebirds of friendship,
of L♡VE and delight.

Bluebirds of happiness,
Bluebirds in flight...

I Wish You Bluebirds

In the WINTER,
When it blows and snows,
May bluebirds cheer you
And snowflakes melt on your nose...

May somebody knit you
A scarf for your chin...

and when it's too cold
to go out and sled...

And mittens to keep
Your pennies in.

A
T

May you have hot chocolate
And a warm cozy bed.

In the SPRINGTIME,
After the showers,
May bluebirds of daydreams
Bring crowds of bright flowers...

And mittens to keep
Your pennies in.

And when it's too cold
To go out and sled...

And when the March winds
Whistle and cry...

May your kite go up
To the top of the sky!

Through all of the seasons,
When bluebirds call,
May yours be the moments
Most cherished of all...

And always I wish you
Bluebirds above
And very special people
To love.